BLAH BLAH BLAH

A Snarky Guide to Office Lingo

SENSORY
LOGIC

This book is dedicated . . .

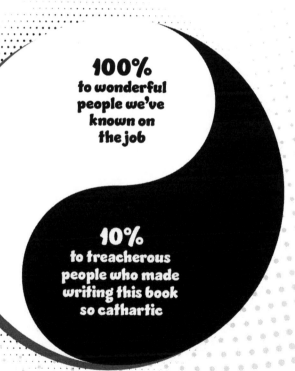

100%
to wonderful
people we've
known on
the job

10%
to treacherous
people who made
writing this book
so cathartic

Sensory Logic Books
www.SensoryLogic.com
1509 Marshall St., N.E., Suite 400
Minneapolis, MN 55413 USA

BLAH, BLAH, BLAH: A Snarky Guide to Office Lingo
Copyright 2021 by Daniel A. Hill
With Howard Moskowitz

Publisher's Cataloging-In-Publication Data
(Prepared by The Donohue Group, Inc.)

Names: Hill, Dan, 1959- author. | Moskowitz, Howard R., author. | Bernthal, Karen, illustrator.
Title: Blah, blah, blah : a snarky guide to office lingo / [Dan Hill and Howard Moskowitz, with plenty of help from friends] ; [book's interior images by Karen Bernthal].

Description: Minneapolis, MN : Sensory Logic, [2021]

Identifiers: ISBN 9780999741658 (softcover)

Subjects: LCSH: Corporate culture—Terminology—Humor. | Business communication—Humor. | LCGFT: Humor. | BISAC: HUMOR / Topic / Business & Professional. | BUSINESS & ECONOMICS / Workplace Culture. | BUSINESS & ECONOMICS / Organizational Behavior. | BUSINESS & ECONOMICS / Business Communication / General.

Classification: LCC HD58.7 .H55 2021 PN6231.B85 | DDC 302.35 818.5402—dc23

Printed in the United States of America

Book cover by *the*BookDesigners
Book's interior design by James Monroe Design LLC
Book's interior images by Karen Bernthal and James Monroe Design LLC

Contents

Preface

As much a fan of *Dilbert* and *The Office* as I am, is this book anti-capitalism? No way, even if CAPITALISM really means: 1) Theft with lawyers in tow. 2) A sacrificial ancient religion that the Haves invoke, along with small bribes, to cajole the Have-Nots to cooperate. After all, who likes UNEMPLOYMENT: No longer getting paid to suffer.

Just as Dilbert and Steve Carell's Michael Scott have colleagues so, too, is *Blah, Blah, Blah* populated by familiar characters. Let's start with yourself given all the foibles on display as you go from getting hired, to tired, to finally being fired. Then add your boss, co-workers, and executives whose dumb strategies leave you vulnerable. Finally, in chapter five I'll introduce the various bit-players in this drama, from departments like HR and Legal to outside vendors.

Yes, go ahead and blame capitalism for being bamboozled yet again. Only there's a more obvious target closer at hand: human nature. We're not logical so much as *psycho-logical* beings, a fact that even academics—aka the landless gentry—have belatedly come around to exploring.

Consider for instance BEHAVIORAL ECONOMICS: 1) The recognition that rather than being like Mr. Spock from *Star Trek,* people really behave more like Homer Simpson from *The Simpsons.* 2) An academic field beset by experts busy thinking through the feelings they would be having if they weren't so busy analyzing them instead.

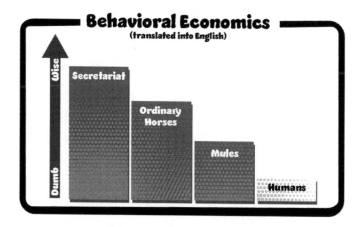

My philosophy is pretty simple: don't be evil and enjoy as many good jokes and friends as possible. On that note, my thanks to Howard Moskowitz (who provided so many entries it seemed only fair to make him a co-author) and to the other friends whose contributions likewise helped to make this book a labor of love.

P.S. To access bonus content—including some useful Tips & Tactics for tackling the tough business issues subject to jokes in this book—please go to sensorylogic.com/blahblahblah/bonus.

YOUR
OWN
FOIBLES

Overthinking Your Job Search

JOB INTERVIEW: An exercise in which a job candidate tries desperately to impress a hiring manager who only wants to know whether the candidate is a jerk.

IMPOSTER SYNDROME: The anxiety experienced by truly qualified people afraid they will never measure up to the confederacy of dunces awaiting them.

PRACTICE INTERVIEW: Hoping the person who agrees to this tedium will overlook the sacrifice and find you a job so that you don't have to do so yourself.

RESUME: The highest form of literary fiction, followed by Letters of Reference.

RESUME STAIN: Even in the great recounting of the journey from swamp to bubbling swamp, a stop along the way too gruesome to admit to anyone—especially one's potential new boss.

Relying on Search Firms

HEADHUNTERS: Matchmakers pairing the wretched with the reckless.

HEAD SHUNTING: When a company hires a headhunter, on the sly, to get one of senior management's losing numbers onto some other company's bingo card.

(overlooked) SOFT SKILLS: Honesty, decency, humility, courage, thoughtfulness, et cetera.

TALENT: The assumption that corporate life reaches Hollywood standards, when it's really more like vaudeville.

TALENT SCOUTING: Looking for people one can praise to the sky while low-balling them when it comes to getting paid.

Trusting in Your Benefits Package

CALLOUSNESS: The pre-existing condition of whoever authorized the company's healthcare plan.

(the) COMPANY HEALTH PLAN: Option C is worse than B, which is worse than A, which is worse than C.

401(k): A financial benefit engineered by law, donated by the employee, matched by the corporation on occasion, and a never-ending source of revenue for financial advisors.

PENSION (fund): 1) See MODEL-T. 2) An archaic form of giving security to an employee in exchange for a lifetime of devotion. Based on the inconvenient assumption that reciprocity is noble. 3) Nowadays, a piggy bank to be raided so a company can repurchase shares of stock.

PERKS: The haves the have-nots don't have.

Seeing the World through Rose-Colored Glasses

ANTICIPATION: 1) The naivete that precedes Anticipointment. 2) The appetizer when disaster is on the menu.

EARLY BIRD: How an optimist describes being an insomniac.

OPTIMISM: 1) A mental programming code that overwrites reality. 2) Trusting in assumptions, i.e., that which is supposedly certain to happen despite absolutely no proof.

STONE-FACED: The way a supervisor or any of one's older colleagues looks at a person gushing about how much fun the corporate outing was this year.

(seeking a) WORK/LIFE BALANCE: 1) The technology sector's most mythical unicorn. 2) An elusive ideal, now recognized to be unachievable—especially for women. 3) What one gets after being fired.

Seeking to Improve Your Abilities On-Site

KNOWLEDGE TRANSFER: The sharing or dissemination of knowledge from people who don't yet know what they're talking about to other people who won't ever really know or care.

ON-THE-JOB TRAINING: Access to thousands of unorganized hours of content for you to wade through on your own.

TALENT DEVELOPMENT: Management's strategy of retaining the employees with the greatest potential by teaching them everything possible about disappointment and regrets.

TRAINING: 1) Classes with three types of attendees: prisoners (those who don't want to be there), vacationers (those who are happy to get away from their desks), and a few eager beavers (those who like to gnaw on information). 2) A sleep disorder remedy. 3) A tragedy with a happy ending thanks to mind-numbing sessions that eventually run out the clock.

WORKSHOPS: The business equivalent of school field trips.

Being a Know-It-All

THE PURSUIT OF KNOWLEDGE

LIFE-LONG LEARNING:
San Quentin University.

TUITION REIMBURSEMENT:
Paying employees to ignore what they learned in school.

SENIORITY:
The point in one's career when one knows next-to-everything about *nothing.*

Turning to Conferences & Formal Learning

FRAMED DIPLOMAS: $100,000 pieces of collectible, autographed artwork.

MBA (Masters of Business Administration): 1) Mediocre But Arrogant. 2) Management By Autocracy, i.e., a workplace paradigm that substitutes esoteric and irrelevant training for common sense, ability, and plenty of hands-on experience.

NOVELTY ITEMS: Swag given away to attendees on checking-in at business conferences so they can immediately grow accustomed to getting something worthless for their money.

ROCK STAR: Being celebrated as a one-hit wonder by a tone-deaf conference organizer.

VIRTUAL CONFERENCES: One's computer, tablet or smartphone screen serving as a fish tank in which piranhas, goldfish, and minnows all dart in and out of their presentations.

Thinking Thought Leaders Will Help You Get Ahead

BUSINESS BOOKS: If not a halfway decent business article repeating itself ad nauseum, then too often a business card consisting of 200-plus pages with one main message: *buy my services, please.*

EARLY ADOPTERS: 1) The people who actually believed *The 4-Hour Workweek* when they (skim)read it. 2) Salespeople who like to blame "the technology" when they miss their numbers. 3) Those who are first into the pool, no matter how deep the water, because they've never heard that bravery and stupidity look the same until the results come in.

FOLLOWERS: Those who believe in various online prophets modeled on traveling medicine men from the 19th century.

MOVING THE CHEESE: A gratuitous reference to a best-selling management book about dealing with change. Another example of *have you read any good book covers lately* because, frankly, who relishes Velveeta® cheese?

THOUGHT LEADER(S): 1) A person who possesses neither any original thoughts nor a propensity to lead. 2) How the speakers at a conference all get described, each one framing an unnecessarily contrarian point of view as somehow revolutionary in nature. 3) What you should consider calling your boss if you're about to ask for a raise.

Practicing Emotional Intelligence Half-Heartedly

ADVICE: Worthless unless it comes from your own mouth.

ALTRUISM: Doing good for somebody while secretly hoping somebody else captures the act on video so it can go viral.

GUILT: A luxury item that one decides is extra baggage after helping to send a colleague packing.

EMPATHY: 1) The experience of thinking you know what someone else is feeling when you really have no idea. 2) A recourse for rationally-oriented product designers when they don't have data to justify a choice. 3) In business, the eighth deadly sin; a capacity deemed antithetical to participating successfully in the sport of career-ladder climbing. 4) The feeling you have for a colleague who has been fired, while you kept your job. In more advanced corporate prototypes, an instinct optimized to disappear within a day or two to make room for fear.

SERENITY: Giving your boss two weeks' notice, effective ten days ago.

Being Too Impulsive & Scatter-Brained

AHEAD-OF-THE-CURVE: 1) A place you always want to be but never are. 2) A polite way to say you failed.

(lots of) BALLS IN THE AIR: The result of lacking the competency to catch any of them.

EMBARASSMENT: 1) How you feel right after pressing Reply All. 2) The feeling of getting caught unprepared at a meeting and accidentally blurting out the truth.

EVOLVING: Totally lost.

SHORT-CIRCUIT: Making the judgment error faster, in the spirit of today.

Bending the Rules

BREAKING DOWN SILOS: The excuse to go talk to a sexy person in another department.

FRATERNIZATION: Poor judgement exercised twice over: first, falling in love; and second, with somebody who likewise joined the wrong company.

INTERNET SURFING: Represents the 80 when the 80/20 rule gets applied to office life.

OFFICE SUPPLIES: Not much like robbing Fort Knox, but it will have to do.

SEXUAL MISCONDUCT: After-hours behavior at conferences, forgetting that what happens in Vegas doesn't stay in Vegas; it appears on one's credit card statement four weeks later.

Being Too Candid

BACK TALK: Verging on the truth.

BEHIND THE EIGHT BALL: Thanks to having been the first to speak, thereby letting the other fools off the hook.

(it's not) BRAIN SURGERY: Trying to explain a simple concept to executives suddenly unable to fathom a course of action which may have some risk and which they're, therefore, loathe to be associated with.

HONESTY: A highly desirable quality admired in the abstract.

YES-MEN: In the evolution of corporate Homo sapiens, a type that's proven far more common than the nearly extinct "maybe, let-me-think-about-it" variant.

Ingratiating Yourself
(a Little Too Obviously)

BROWN-NOSING: What it often takes to earn brownie points.

BUTTERING UP: Flattering your boss while you still have an appetite for corporate life.

EAR CANDY: A smart way to feed a boss hungry for praise.

EPIC: How to describe your manager's latest presentation if you're seeking a promotion.

JUMP THE SHARK: An effort to bolster your relevance that takes its name from a 1970s comedy sketch involving a pair of water skis and everyone's favorite business guru, Henry "The Fonz" Winkler.

Being Too Ravenous

WHAT ARE YOU REALLY HUNGRY FOR?
(Food or Appreciation)

APPETITE:
What you had before
you entered the
company cafeteria.

A SEAT AT THE TABLE:
The desire to be part of meetings
which, if achieved, is instantly
regretted given the childish
incompetency shown
by the adults already there.

Being Insufficiently Subservient

ATTITUDE: 1) What employees are told they have in spades on being reprimanded. 2) That which is dangerous to have and impossible to avoid having given enough time on the job.

CONTRARIAN: The opportunity to reduce next month's payroll by another person.

PRECISION: 1) Correcting a mistake your boss happened to make. 2) Subsequently, cleaning out your desk within the allotted two minutes.

PUSHBACK: The instant gratification that *former* employees got by saying "No" to their supervisors.

REBEL: The main draw at a corporate hanging.

Burning Your Bridges

BEEN THERE, DONE THAT: 1) A saying favored by people who no longer attend meetings, return phone calls or cope with the reality that what they deem absurd is likely to happen. 2) Workers who are basically like hot-air balloons floating lazily overhead.

CAREER SUICIDE: Reading or even acknowledging this book exists.

DOMINANCE: Imagining oneself enshrined in Cooperstown after a career of bunting every pitch.

EYE-ROLLING: Career-limiting corporate body language, with outbreaks especially common during long staff meetings.

REPRISAL: Your manager's response after you give a really good presentation and forget to mention that your best ideas were the result of superior coaching.

Coasting along

ENERGETIC: The first stage in a new employee's journey that proceeds to narcolepsy and, finally, to being a victim of right-sizing.

PHONING IT IN: Made even easier by texting instead.

REMOTE: A way to describe the motivation level of people during a virtual meeting that they attend in their underwear or pajamas, multitask throughout the call, and still get credit for attending.

REPURPOSING: Transforming lethargy into sloth as one of next year's "stretch" goals.

TIME MANAGEMENT: Tracking one's (potential) activity, conceptually speaking of course.

Ducking (Any Further) Responsibilities

EXCUSES: 1) Willpower getting the sniffles. 2) The opposite of INCUSES, which are excuses that arrive in your in-box and preclude you from using them yourself, thereby challenging your creativity.

I'M SWAMPED: 1) The modern way to boast of one's value and heroic self-sacrifice on behalf of the company. 2) Recognizing one's natural habitat. 3) The go-to line of someone who is busy with busy work.

JOBFUSCATE: Ensuring your boss doesn't understand what's on your plate in terms of work assignments, nor how little progress you're making on any of them.

(above my) PAY GRADE: What Karl Marx failed to anticipate as the rallying cry of workers the world over.

PROBLEM-SOLVING: Ignoring the problem until you go away.

Battling Fear

ADVANCED: What you call the evolution of something you used to understand but no longer do.

DAMAGE CONTROL: The work week's true agenda.

LOSS AVERSION: Limiting mistakes by squandering opportunities.

PRETHINK: 1) Before the big meeting, holding a smaller meeting comprised of those with the most to lose. 2) Sterilizing fear.

UPSIDE: What one hopes one won't have to hope for.

Getting Stressed out

GRINDING TO A HALT

Default Option

1. The option for those without options.

2. Thinking inside a smaller box than usual.

WORK STOPPAGES: TAKING ASPIRIN.

Barely Coping (Did You Jump or Were You Pushed?)

BETWEEN A ROCK AND A HARD PLACE: 1) Walking into the office every day. 2) Another way to describe the struggle to achieve a work/life balance.

BURNING THE CANDLE AT BOTH ENDS: 1) In between going to the office while it's still dark and leaving the office after it's dark again, staying busy keeping your boss in the dark. 2) A way to cast light on one's exact location BETWEEN A ROCK AND A HARD PLACE.

DEBRIEF: The meeting prior to going home to cry and drown your sorrow in your desired vice.

RESILIENCE: 1) The latest way of saying "Sh*t happens." 2) Being able to tolerate the same stupid stuff day after day.

WORK SPASM: Getting so bored on the job that, for a change of pace, you decide to do some real work.

Actively Disengaging

ABSENTEEISM: A chronic preference to be any place other than at work, despite drawing a salary that means you're being bribed to be there.

COMMUTING: 1) Spending time, effort, and gas money in racing to work, only to stall out upon arrival. 2) The daily, two-way re-enactment of what used to be a one-way trip to the gallows.

MANUAL LABOR: The reason for taking the soul-sucking office job one has now.

PASSION: The impetus one needs to go to work . . . and later to make a career change.

REASONS TO CARE: N/A.

Recognizing the End of the Road a Little Too Late

DEADWOOD: The other people being fired, not oneself, who was fired by mistake.

LUNCH BREAK: 1) Sharing a meal with your smart phone. 2) A midday interlude enjoyed by those who will be unexpectedly looking for a new job soon.

(the end of) SHELF LIFE: Technical skills in 18 months.

WE'RE TAKING YOU OFF THIS PROJECT FOR A MORE IMPORTANT ONE: Emptying your desk.

YOU'RE FIRED: The bittersweet sound of needing to find another place to work with kinder office politics.

YOUR
MANAGER'S
BLIND SPOTS

A Haphazard Approach to Adding Staff

BACKGROUND CHECK: Taking a second look at the job candidate's photo (assuming there is one).

GETTING CONSIDERED: 1) Leaving job candidates in the uncomfortable state of not knowing why they will be ultimately rejected for the job. 2) Giving job candidates 500+ milliseconds of attention.

LET'S SQUARE THE CIRCLE: Encouraging the HR department to add a geometry test to the job interview process.

(seeking a) PROVEN TEAM PLAYER: 1) Someone pliable and willing to cover all or part of colleagues' workloads. 2) Well versed in the greater task of sweeping things under the rug.

VIDEO INTERVIEWING: Swipe right on the camera.

Onboarding Ambiguity & Downright Misinformation

ACCESSIBLE: The promise made by an employee's new boss the day that person is hired, on the assumption the employee will be wise enough never to take it for a test drive.

(the promise of) AUTONOMY: Being micro-managed only part-time.

DIRECT REPORTS: In a company's organizational chart, staff members linked to their boss by a solid line intersected by an image of the Berlin Wall they're stuck behind.

HYBRID WORKPLACE: A breakthrough model that enables employees to be productive in the office, at home or elsewhere, thereby combining being semi-neglected with total responsibility for progress.

MATRIX STRUCTURE: 1) A case of some individuals reporting to more than one supervisor or leader. These relationships take the form of either a solid line, a dotted line, a loosely dash-dotted line, an erased line, or forgotten deadlines that lead to joining the breadline. 2) A double helix of ever fainter question marks stretching off into the horizon.

Pretending to Be Helpful

DELIVERABLES: Stuff that goes from your manager's to-do list onto yours.

ETA (Estimated Time of Arrival): Piloting a project on which one's boss proves to be the hijacker.

FACIPULATE: 1) A combination of "facilitate" and "manipulate." 2) Managers pretending to operate mental forklifts.

HEADS-UP: Incoming artillery.

(the) STAFF: A group that follows its manager's instructions but still gets the work done.

More Than a Little Tone Deaf

APPRECIATION: A word that causes your boss to stutter.

DIALOGUE: Two people discussing a problem in the way the boss wants and that the company would approve of.

(let's get our) DUCKS IN A ROW: The admonishment of a supervisor who favors flying in an "I" rather than a "V" formation.

EMERGENCY MEETING: Your clueless manager buttonholing you right before you're about to leave for a long weekend. Why? So the two of you can discuss department-wide problems that have been festering for half a decade.

(being) ON-MESSAGE: Having a point to make, no matter how tedious or false.

Deliberately Hard of Hearing

PUT IT IN WRITING: So I don't have to hear about, nor read, your suggestion.

WAYS TO SHUT DOWN A CONVERSATION

"First, let me say"

"you're being too emotional"

"With all due respect"

"To be perfectly honest"

"At the end of the day"

Is a Real Gasbag

ACTUALLY: What's actually said when there's actually very little to actually say.

CAN'T EMPHASIZE ENOUGH: Yes, you *certainly* can.

GONE ARE THE DAYS: Of fourscore and seven years ago, when business wasn't a 24/7 proposition.

IMPACTFUL: The adjectival version of a muscle car.

THUS: A word used in pedantic emails to remind the recipient who's the boss.

Sometimes Oblivious to How Haste Makes Waste

ACTION ITEM: What you're told is really important, even though your boss will forget about it tomorrow.

LET'S GET OUT IN FRONT OF THIS: Oncoming bus.

PRO-ACTIVE: 1) Charging into battle on a sawhorse. 2) Making preparations for the error ahead of time, rather than making the error spontaneously.

RE-ALLOCATING: 1) Half-way to acknowledging a mistake has been made. 2) Letting your staff know they dug the trench in the wrong place.

URGENT: 1) Maybe. 2) Time-sensitive requests from bosses who can't effectively manage their own time. 3) Something you forgot to tell someone three weeks ago.

Other Times Prefers a Snail's Pace

(we'll practice) AN ABUNDANCE OF CAUTION: Progress will be made only by accident.

BEHIND SCHEDULE: What management says when the project is progressing at the pace that the engineers said it would and nobody listened.

BOIL THE OCEAN: A term inadvertently coined by the humorist Will Rogers during World War One when asked what to do about German U-Boat aggression. Nowadays, a reference to overthinking impossible tasks that weren't originally thought out at all.

SPEED: The *bête noire* of middle managers, whose job it is to do things slowly as a way to keep their jobs.

TIMELINE: 1) The first line drawn on a white board, typically by managers wanting to feel like they've contributed to the meeting. 2) A process that starts with assigning responsibility and ends with excuse-making.

Favors the Mirage of Progress

BY WAY OF HOUSEKEEPING: Making sure at the start of a project's kick-off meeting that everyone knows the agenda and, more importantly, where the snacks are kept.

COSMETIC CHANGES: When something should be massively re-done.

DEADLINE: An artificial date by which to accomplish an irrelevant task.

MOVING THE NEEDLE: Acupuncture, corporate style.

QUICK WINS: Building momentum to ensure the eventual car crash is fatal.

An Expert at Incompetency

(finding the) KEY TAKEAWAYS: Adept at separating the junk from the trash in a report.

LET'S SOCIALIZE THIS: A supervisor who believes sharing the blame is better than risking success.

MANAGER: An air-traffic controller unaided by radar.

MEANDERTHAL: A boss, usually of the older and heavier male variety, known to pontificate aimlessly.

TEE IT UP: Said by a boss whose talent level is a perfect fit for miniature golf.

Indulges in the Myth of Quality Control

ACCURACY: 1) When quarterly targets are missed by exactly the amount expected. 2) Measuring the wrong things well or the right things badly.

BEST PRACTICES: The stage of organizational development just prior to COST-CUTTING, i.e., the opportunity to beggar thy neighbor in a socially acceptable way.

GRANULAR: Anal.

LET'S PUT LIPSTICK ON THIS PIG: 1) Putting a favorable spin on a product or service offering everyone knows won't bring home the bacon. 2) The precursor to swine flu. Symptoms typically include the loss of both perspective and income. 3) Having engineers wear ties for the presentation.

QUALITY: 1) The increasingly rare ability to make an item which outlasts the credit card payments required to own it outright. 2) Often a topic included in a survey, done in lieu of a deeper understanding of that same topic.

Grants Self-Amnesty

CLOSING THE LOOP: 1) The steps taken to ensure that the only people who know the extent of your screwup have been fired, promoted or otherwise dispatched. 2) A non-decision on a non-issue by non-entities waiting for lunch.

CLOSING THE LOOP AT WORK

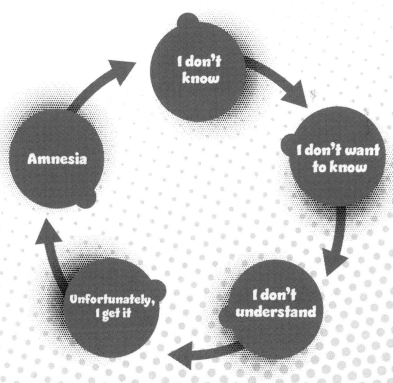

I don't know

I don't want to know

I don't understand

Unfortunately, I get it

Amnesia

Imposes a CRAZY Work Schedule

DISTRACTIONS: How an overly ambitious boss views an employee's beloved family.

(going the) EXTRA MILE: 1) A supervisor's excuse for ruining one's evening, weekend or vacation, and eventually one's entire life. 2) Working overtime for a free slice of pizza. 3) Still running after you've crossed a project's finish line.

LAPTOP COMPUTER: The equivalent of an electronic bracelet that keeps you from becoming a flight risk from after-hours' assignments.

OVERTIME: 1) From the employees' perspective, part of a work week lasting from 41 to 120 hours and the prerequisite to proving one's worth to the company. 2) From management's perspective, the desire to be paid extra for still not doing the work. 3) From shareholders' perspective, the time it takes to sign the latest dividend check and deposit it in a bank nearby.

PRACTICIDE: A business plan designed to kill you from overwork.

VACATION (OR HOLIDAY): A beautiful setting where one goes with loved ones to reduce one's daily workload to only three or four hours a day.

WEEKEND EMAIL THREADS: Shame on God for resting on the seventh day.

WORKDAY: An eight-hour stretch of time lasting approximately eleven hours in all.

WORKING LATE IN THE OFFICE: But only on the days that end in "y."

WORK SMARTER: 1) A reminder that the day doesn't technically end until midnight. 2) A really annoying phrase used by arrogant managers to convey their complete ignorance of *everything*.

Creates a High-Stress Environment

ASAP (As Soon as Possible): Always Sparking A Panic.

GRIEF: A feeling now rebranded as GOOD GRIEF.

HITTING A WALL: Monday afternoons.

HOPE YOU'RE WELL-RESTED FROM YOUR VACATION: 1) Hell awaits. 2) The prospect of pumping oxygen into the company by leaving you out of breath.

JOY: A word that infiltrates the office by appearing on a few Christmas cards.

(the) OFFICE: The movie set for a dystopian film.

PRESSURE: Unhealthy levels of stress, kept in check by managers successfully failing to notice how their staffs really feel.

SENSE OF URGENCY: The translation of "someday" into "now" for anybody who still wants to be employed tomorrow.

SUPPLY-AND-DEMAND: 1) An intricate and complicated business theory that, when boiled down, translates into whatever the boss *demands* staff *supplies*. 2) A saying made famous by Adam Smith in regards to the shuffling of market forces being enacted by an Invisible Hand (when it's not busy beating off).

24/7: 1) The expected availability of employees after being provided with laptops and mobile phones by their companies. 2) An effort in numbers to convey an attitude which exists more in fantasy and hope than in reality.

Always Needs to Be Right

CHECK THE BOX: The ultimate victory of those who would substitute process for reality.

CRITICAL THINKING SKILLS: The ability to stoutly defend a judgment arrived at prior to analyzing the facts.

FACT-FINDING MISSION: 1) A systematic, formal application of the Confirmation Bias principle. 2) The R & D conducted after a new product launch has tanked, as part of a desperate quest for evidence that will support unsupportable findings.

INFORMED DECISIONS: 1) A boss's gut feelings. 2) Further evidence that the biggest lies in life are the ones we tell ourselves.

UNBIASED ADVICE: What your boss confidently believes is fact, even though your colleagues are sure it's something the boss just made up.

Pushes Weight around

HERE ARE SOME RESUMES JUST FOR YOUR FILES: A way of putting an employee seeking a raise on notice.

HOW CAN I MAKE THIS JOB MORE INTERESTING TO YOU: Your boss all but asking whether it might be easier to simply order a body bag.

KILLING IT: Your boss absolutely, categorically over-estimating his or her prowess.

LET'S PUT THIS INTO CONTEXT: Here's why you're wrong.

WILL YOU BE IN ALL WEEK: I've got this albatross I'm looking to offload.

Want to Leave It All behind?

INTERFACING: In tomorrow's fully automated economy, two robots having a tete-a-tete. For now, a robotic way of saying you've been asked to sit down with your boss for a "friendly" face-to-face chat.

FOUR WAYS to ESCAPE your BOSS

Family Leave

Medical Leave

1

2

3

4

Taking leave of your senses

Binge watching Leave It to Beaver at home

Derails People's Careers

BONUS: 1) The reward given for being lucky enough to participate in the group defining the rules for authorizing bonuses. 2) Money not yet stolen that must be somehow accounted for.

CAREER LADDER: The promise of promotion placed dangerously close to electrical wiring.

DEAD-END JOB: Employment without deployment.

EXEMPT EMPLOYEE: Ensuring that employees work *long and hard* but are only compensated for the *hard* part.

REASSIGNED: Put on a glide-path to oblivion.

Likes to Cajole or Coerce Staff

ACHIEVEMENT (will be justly rewarded): Something done successfully, often by stepping upon the heads of those fortunate enough to work beneath the achiever.

(let me) CHIME IN: A musical way of interrupting a subordinate or a disgraced colleague.

HEAVY LIFTING: Being muscled into handling a difficult assignment alone on the basis that others lack the strength to help out.

PEP TALK: The boss's second-to-last motivational strategy, just ahead of "Coming down on you like a ton of bricks."

SUPPORT FUNCTION: The person who does the real work reasonably well, allowing the boss to maintain a high level of ineptitude.

THIS IS WHERE THE RUBBER MEETS THE ROAD: A manager inadvertently urging the staff to quit their jobs and move on.

VOLUNTEERED: 1) Punishing the people who didn't attend the staff meeting because they were busy doing real work. 2) A version of *voluntold*, which is what the boss does when no one volunteers for an impossible task.

WORDSMITH IT: Because I can't spell, despite earning well north of $100k a year.

YOU'RE REALLY GOOD WITH PEOPLE: A manager signaling that when it comes to a certain odious colleague, you're now the go-between.

WE: You.

Keen on Controlling Behavior

COLORING OUTSIDE THE LINES: The corporate version of why the nuns slapped one's hands in first grade.

FOLLOW THE RULES: Even if they change hourly.

MICRO-MANAGING: 1) Invisible leg irons. 2) Sweating the little stuff because the big picture is cloudy. 3) What a diminutive boss is best at.

RIDING HERD: An attempt by micro-managing administrators to portray themselves as free-range cowboys running cattle. (If that analogy doesn't tell you pretty much all you need to know about how these people view their direct reports, then you're not paying attention.)

(stay in your) SWIMLANE: Welcome to the kiddy pool.

Keen on Controlling Ideas

ALIGNMENT: A rookie mistake, failing to recognize that being asked "to align" on something by a manager really means "to fall into line."

(strictly) BY THE NUMBERS: A strategy for managers to use in curtailing options, limiting exploration, and simultaneously introducing biased, questionable data.

CARTE BLANCHE: 1) A French term meaning blank document, loosely translated to mean the freedom to make any and all decisions. 2) Proof that France doesn't practice capitalism.

COMPLAINT: 1) The misguided first step taken by somebody who wants to understand why your way is better. 2) A synonym for IMPASSE.

CONSENSUS: A general agreement as to what the boss's opinion is.

Is Ego-Centric (in Both a Left- and Right-Brained Way)

CONTROL: Establishing one's own incompetency, rather than acquiescing to somebody else's.

I'M IN CHARGE HERE

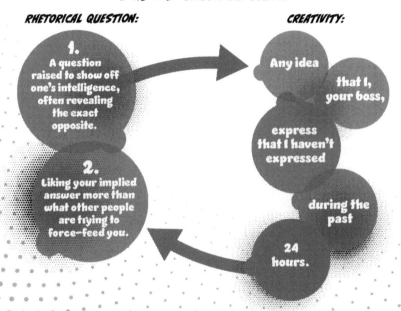

RHETORICAL QUESTION:

1. A question raised to show off one's intelligence, often revealing the exact opposite.

2. Liking your implied answer more than what other people are trying to force-feed you.

CREATIVITY:

Any idea that I, your boss, express that I haven't expressed during the past 24 hours.

Adverse to Change

FILE DRAWER: The final resting place of ideas not enacted immediately.

IN THE PIPELINE: The elongated version of a BLACK HOLE.

MIDDLE MANAGEMENT: Where the good ideas stop.

NEW: Relaunching the reproduction of a revitalized retread.

SUGGESTION BOX: Often conveniently located in the employee breakroom next to the trash bin.

Is Dictatorial by Nature

BOSS: See BULLY.

BULLY: See BOSS.

COMMAND-AND-CONTROL: The method of governing a department otherwise known as a participatory dictatorship, with one person doing the dictating and the rest participating.

DO MORE WITH LESS: Since people can live for roughly three weeks without food, three days without water, and three minutes without air, telling your staff to figure out what else can be learned about the limits of human endurance.

HARD CHARGING: A supervisor's self-congratulatory description for being an unmuzzled pit bull.

Comfortable Creating Discomfort

EMOJIS: The feelings you would be having at work if they were allowed.

(we'll) NEED TO FINESSE THIS: You've joined a suicide mission.

PRODUCTIVITY: Sweat and blood measured in dollars and cents.

TOXIC WORK ENVIRONMENTS: A chance for OSHA and the EPA to team up.

UNDER THE WIRE: The nimble version of living life under the gun.

Always Looking for Someone to Blame

ACCOUNTABILITY: A risk that grows exponentially the lower you are on the totem pole.

(the) FACT OF THE MATTER IS: 1) A handsome lie told by an accuser of higher rank in the act of punishing or terminating an employee of lower rank. 2) An opportunity for creative blaming by novices still learning how to blame and not yet fully adept in the art of being a boss.

FALL GUY: The value of adding people to the project team.

SETTING THE RECORD STRAIGHT: 1) One's own lie versus somebody else's. 2) "Yes, it's my fault . . . but let's not get overly-technical here."

WHO'S HANDLING THIS: 1) Where's my fall guy? 2) Even more direct is I THOUGHT *YOU* WERE HANDLING THIS, i.e., one of us is in trouble, namely you because "I have to run to another meeting."

Biased, Off-Base Feedback & Appraisals

ABILITY: What you had when originally hired.

I'M CONFUSED: About whether you're really that dumb or not.

KEEP UP THE GOOD WORK: 1) "Thanks for making me look good. Now about that promotion, let's talk again maybe next year." 2) The articulated version of "Nice job today, but we both know you're slipping."

PERFORMANCE IMPROVEMENT PLAN: 1) From a manager's perspective, what happens when HR says I can't fire you. 2) From the employee's perspective, a quarter's worth of work that suddenly needs to be accomplished in 30 days as a way of putting me on notice.

RECOGNITION: Anytime a boss is not chewing out a subordinate.

Gives Critiques That Disregard Others

ANNUAL PERFORMANCE REVIEWS: 1) The third rail of office life. 2) As an employee, a document I write myself and that my boss either agrees or disagrees with after skim-reading it.

GENEROUS: A supervisor the day before retirement.

KEY PERFORMANCE INDICATORS (KPIs): 1) Mysterious numbers used to browbeat the inattentive, intimidate the innumerate, and elevate the mediocre. 2) Evidence that one's making the company money, customer satisfaction be damned.

360-DEGREE ASSESSMENTS: Input that provides an opportunity to correct misperceptions, i.e., "Well, Bob, I think people might mistake your general mediocrity for extreme incompetence."

UNDERPERFORMING: Found wanting by those who want you gone.

THREE

COLLEAGUES STIRRING THE POT

Being Ignored or Backdoored

ASKHOLE: A person who keeps asking for your advice but never follows it.

COMMON GROUND: No man's land.

GIVING YOU A HEADS UP: That I've already gone around you.

OUT OF THE LOOP: A blessing until it isn't.

TAKING THE CONVERSATION OFFLINE: Privatizing communication because I can get something out of this conversation that I don't want to share with others.

Difficult, Unsatisfying Interactions

ACTIVE LISTENING: A colleague preparing to interrupt.

DECEPTIONIST: An executive assistant or anybody else whose job entails suffocating your requests with a smile.

DRILL DOWN: Fracking through thick skulls in the belief that there is actually something of value below the surface.

REVISIT: A gathering of the stupid, the slow to understand, the slow to keep up, and the slow to give up and leave well enough alone.

VIRTUAL WORK TEAMS: 1) Colleagues who alternate between talking over one another and realizing nobody has anything to say. 2) Over time, the sensation that you've been binge-watching the game show *Hollywood Squares*.

Versions of Phone Hell

CAN EVERYONE PLEASE MUTE THEIR PHONES: Feeling as if you've bought a condo in the Tower of Babel.

PIN CODE: When it comes to joining a conference call, a bridge to nowhere.

SCREENING MY CALLS: 1) "No" in advance. 2) I'm actually no longer employed. Therefore, I'm not in the office anymore and pick up my emails from home, dressed in my underwear. 3) A request for you to learn how to text.

THIS MAILBOX IS FULL: 1) Passive-aggressive loners pretending to be popular, in-demand, and fully engaged by their work. 2) A Potemkin Village imitation of what being productively busy looks like. 3) Often a clue that the owner of the phone number is over 50 years of age.

VOICE MAIL: 1) Avoidance-enabling technology. 2) An archaic form of voice communication primarily retained to ruin one's first day back from vacation.

Opportunities to Spin, Deflect, Hint or Hold Back

(the) ELEPHANT IN THE ROOM: The foot-long bong visible on the shelf behind the boss's desk during a zoom meeting.

GOOD TO PUT A FACE TO THE NAME: Finally meeting the idiot with whom you've been exchanging messages for months.

I'LL GET BACK TO YOU: 1) The formal, courteous version of "Don't call us, we'll call you." Other forms include "It's been fun and real but it hasn't been real fun" and "Uh, that would be a no." 2) The absence of "Yes" x time. 3) A white lie. See LET'S DO LUNCH (approximately *never*).

LET'S STAY CONNECTED: We'll never talk again.

TOUCHING BASE: 1) Said by people pretending not to be annoyed that they haven't heard from somebody within the past 24 hours. 2) A desire to meet someone for just long enough to get what you need or want.

Trying to Survive Meetings

ALL-DAY MEETING: 1) A badly facilitated one-hour session. 2) An opportunity to learn the maximum amount of obfuscation a meeting room can contain before carbon monoxide fumes overwhelm its occupants.

(the) BOTTOM LINE: The wedgie in your pants from sitting in meetings all day.

DECISION-SNIPER: The person in a staff meeting, often the boss's surrogate, who blows up the group's decision at the last minute, necessitating a follow-up meeting in which nothing gets decided again.

LUNCH PROVIDED: A meeting likely to be so dull that something had to be done to ensure the conference room isn't empty.

STAFF MEETINGS: Tedium interspersed with boredom.

As If Monday Mornings Weren't Tough Enough Already

AGENDA: A list of items to be covered in the meeting so everybody gets on "the same page" of a book nobody will ever read.

Collaborating, Sort of

ALAP (As Late as Possible): Colleagues submitting their initial portion of a project belatedly to avoid getting more assignments too quickly.

BUILDING CONSENSUS: 1) One muffled cry after another. 2) People who would otherwise disagree saying "Yes" before reasoned judgment spots a major error.

COLLABORATING: When you offer ideas that help me get my work done the way I want to do it.

CO-SOURCING: 1) A colleague about to claim credit for your hard work. 2) When the odds of getting a promotion drop to no better than 50/50.

DATA DUMP: 30% of what's in your co-worker's head, written hurriedly on a piece of paper that's entirely indecipherable.

GAINING TRACTION: We've run out of people who make no bones about ignoring us, so now we're on to trying to gain support from people who ignore us in ways we haven't yet figured out.

NICE-TO-HAVE: Something essential to your goals but inconsequential to mine.

PARTNERING: The opportunity to work together well with at least one other person, provided one gets pleasure from doing most of the work.

PICK YOUR BRAIN: A colleague's inner vulture landing on your desk.

REACHING OUT: Getting in touch with someone by email despite knowing you're supposed to call that person to work things out in real time.

The Empty Weight of Teamwork

AVAILABLE: 1) Inevitably, the one person you *don't* really want added to your project team. 2) Horror on hearing your boss volunteer you as well.

CRUNCH TIME: Teaming up to make errors more quickly than usual.

PROJECT LEADER: The one paying for pizza every night the last month of the project.

TEAMWORK: 1) A group of people tasked with achieving a common goal while undermining each other's efforts. 2) Embracing the possibility of blaming others. 3) Activity that exhausts your mental and emotional bandwidth to the extent that you're unable to do any real work.

TEAM SPIRIT: The unfounded belief that the gusto of bonus-eligible managers is shared by the poor schmucks they rely on to deliver results.

Essentially Absentee "Teammates"

CHECKS-AND-BALANCES: How the group that will do *badly* gets saved by the group that wants to do *nothing*.

CO-WORKERS: 1) Those with whom you spend more time than your own family but know less about than a mongoose. 2) A crew of fellow "*until* workers," meaning everyone who half-heartedly works while waiting until any of the following events takes place: a coffee break, bathroom break, lunch, 5 o'clock, sick day, vacation, a new job, or retirement. 3) A professional and respectful term referring to the people whose substandard work you often correct.

GIVING 110%: What people who normally give 50% say when they ramp up to 60%.

JOBSTACLE: Any work-related barrier that gets in the way of getting your work done. See CO-WORKERS.

WFH (Working from Home): The adult version of playing Hide-and-Seek.

Running in Place
(Trying to Innovate Together)

BLEEDING EDGE: The description of those who do things by those who avoid doing any work.

BRAINSTORMING: 1) A meeting in which you're told all ideas are welcome because there aren't any bad ideas—except for the ones you suggest. 2) The ability to present marginally innovative ideas using enough corporate speak that they sound both sexy and daring.

EDGY: A product or process so different from the norm that more time needs to be spent explaining it than putting it to use.

IDEATION: 1) A group process of spontaneously coming up with random ideas the team must then validate on a scale from silly to absurd. 2) For consultants, socializing on the client's budget. 3) For everyone else involved, permission to think without reality effecting the outcome.

LET'S BALLPARK THIS: Why not get out of here after lunch and talk things over at the game?

Inertia & Lethargy (Stuck in the Mud)

IMPLEMENTATION: A fancy way of saying it's finally time to get something done. A step to be followed by a status report whereby "inconclusive" is said many times over in different ways.

IT IS WHAT IT IS: A ritualistic phrase meant to banish the evil spirits inhabiting the company.

POSITIVE SPIN: Motion without forward movement and, as such, the essence of corporate life.

POSTPONING: 1) Always a wise move. 2) Making the mistake tomorrow that one should have made today.

WORKLOAD: Employees' perception of the amount of work on their plates. Generally, a vague, undefined amount meant to convey infinity. See BOATLOAD and SH*TLOAD for guidance.

Encountering Resistance

CHANGE: The Rock before the Hard Place gets defined.

CYA (Cover Your Ass): After trying to think outside the box, feeling better if you're inside it.

GETTING SOME PUSHBACK: Experiencing gale-force winds.

THIS IS HOW WE DID IT LAST YEAR: When I also, strangely, didn't get a pay raise.

WORKING THROUGH THE CHANNELS: Where the cholesterol count is high.

Don't Try This at Home

TEAM-BUILDING EXERCISES BEST AVOIDED

Let's Put Lipstick on This Pig

Awkward

Fatal

Thrown under the Bus

Driving beyond the Headlights

Crazy

Drinking the Kool-Aid®

Boiling the Ocean

Drinking from a Fire Hose

Receiving the Boot

Painful

Sloppy Indifferent Outcomes

BLACK HOLE: The nature of projects handled by those whose primary job is to keep their jobs.

CAUTIOUSLY OPTIMISTIC: We're screwed.

(it) FELL THROUGH THE CRACKS: We only half-tried to accomplish what you had requested, knowing you're too low on the totem pole to worry about.

ORGANIC: 1) Errors that happen naturally, rather than being caused by the imposed incompetency of those higher up in the food chain. 2) A euphemism for "spoiled rotten."

SNAFU (Situation Normal All F*cked Up): 1) A polite acronym to use in the company of those who harbor a low tolerance for profanity, a high need to acknowledge the obvious, and a secret desire to know more military-sounding code words that mean *screw-up*. 2) A playful term that makes a corporate fiasco sound like a small sneeze.

Working the Room (Often to Escape Blame)

BLAMESTORMING: 1) An informal meeting to figure out a viable scapegoat after something goes wrong. 2) The inverse of the Vatican canonizing a saint.

COME-TO-JESUS MEETING: One without much hope of salvation.

PAPER TRAILS: Playing the game of *rock paper scissors* and losing out, having forgotten that in corporate life it's always better to choosing the option that involves making a fist.

SEND ME A CLEAN EMAIL: Write something that I can forward without making us look complicit.

WALLPAPER A MEETING: 1) Ensuring that allies attend a meeting where one's idea is up for a pro forma vote. 2) As an ally dutifully attending said meeting and soon bored to death, recalling what were reportedly Oscar Wilde's last words as he lay dying in a shabby, French provincial hotel: "One of us has to go, me or the wallpaper."

Jockeying for Power (Petty Rivalries)

ACQUAINTANCE: A former friend of yours who just got the coveted promotion.

AMBITIOUS: A desirable quality in direct reports but not in one's peers.

JEALOUSY: The feeling one has about colleagues based on a solid understanding of one's own inadequacies.

POWER HUNGRY: The fatal flaw of a promising rival whose career threatens to get in your way.

RISING STARS: Need to be wary of the darkness surrounding them.

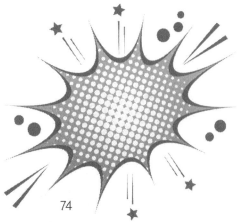

Slander & General Mean-Spiritedness

BACKSTABBING: The essence of office politics, whereby the promise to "have your back" actually means the intended target is clearly in sight.

BORN IN A SILO: A colleague who hasn't taken a shower for three days.

OFFICE GOSSIP: 1) Compared to the company's tardy, after-the-fact email blast announcing the news to rank-and-file employees, the truth catching an earlier, direct flight. 2) Darkness traveling at the speed of light.

POISONING THE WELL: The Kremlin's version of playing office politics.

SPILLING TEA: 1) Divulging something juicy about someone, usually online; see CYBERBULLYING. 2) A version of office politics favored by those who like to watch BBC programming.

Long Live the Myth of Kumbaya

BLESS YOUR HEART: 1) I vehemently disagree with you and expect you to fail. Therefore, I'm not going to do anything to help out. 2) A super polite saying common in the South, where women don't participate in orgies because doing so would require too many thank-you notes.

HALO: Worn by someone without enemies, which is to say newly deceased.

LOYALTY: People "all in" until they're all out to get you.

RIDE SHARING: The right thing for others to do.

(fake) SOCIAL SMILES: Happiness deprived of oxygen.

EXECUTIVE
BLUNDERS

Strategic Mistakes (for Which Somebody Else Must Pay)

ALLIANCE: Two parties to a deal now looking for an excuse to go to war.

DOWNSIZING: 1) The act of growing smaller to fit the imagination of the era. 2) Rechristening the part of the ship that's not already underwater.

MOAT: A term popularized by Warren Buffett to describe ways in which a company might protect itself, forgetting that the Dark Ages have largely drawn to a close.

RIGHT-SIZING: 1) All but admitting the company recklessly expanded too quickly. 2) A round-about way of letting the company's most talented and knowledgeable people go to competitors. 3) Firing people but with a strategic ring to the company's move.

SMALL BUSINESS: What a large corporation becomes by selling assets to "right-size" itself in a competitive environment.

Restructuring Woes

CHAPTER 11: Either the final chapter of a company's official, published history or else the start of a sequel.

COOPETITION: What happens when two companies merge and neither one says "Uncle."

MERGERS AND ACQUISITIONS: 1) A private handshake between two CEOs looking out for their own careers while trying to justify their deal on a commercial basis. 2) Empire building using left-over cement. 3) A business activity that inspired the joke about a CEO who arrives in a place beset by terrible suffering and informs a guard, "I was supposed to go to heaven, not hell." to which the guard replies: "Didn't you hear the news? We merged."

REALIGNMENT: 1) A euphemism used to describe one or more of the following events: mass layoffs, liquidations, a run on the company's stock, and/or the removal of the ping-pong table in the break room. 2) The CEO's limo needs work.

STREAMLINE: 1) Emphasizing what's essential, only to realize that excludes oneself. 2) Getting "back to basics" like reenacting the Hundred Years' War.

Lack of Vision

BIG PICTURE: Here's what *impossible* looks like.

CORNER OFFICE: 1) The epitome of success, providing two views and yet no perspective. 2) Larger in size than most company offices to allow for extra wiggle room.

FIVE-YEAR PLAN: 1) A pleasant fiction that fails to survive even the briefest of encounters with reality. 2) A plan with the half-life of a mosquito.

FLAVOR OF THE MONTH: The latest in a long series of management fads, none of which taste as good as Ben & Jerry's® Chubby Hubby.

PARADIGM SHIFTS: Modeling one's business on earthquakes.

SWOT ANALYSIS: A candid appraisal of the company's current Strengths and Weaknesses as well as the Opportunities and Threats involved in making such an appraisal.

TOP-DOWN LEADERSHIP: 1) An organization where stupidity begins with senior management and trickles down to those who, while less stupid, simply follow orders. 2) Those blessed with the foresight to lead the company to a mountaintop TBD.

TRENDSPOTTING: Guessing what the light at the end of the tunnel might actually be.

VISION: 1) That which is never seen, seldom heard about, and rarely if ever achieved. 2) That which leads to creating a VISION STATEMENT, aka mumble jumble waiting to be bronzed.

WE NEED TO BE STRATEGIC: About when to be clueless.

Just Waiting to Be Foreclosed on

HAUNTED HOUSES

RELOCATION

The company moving its headquarters closer, but not too close, to where the new CEO has bought a mansion.

FAMILY BUSINESS

1) The other place where Freudian drives are actualized, driven by a combination of economic motives and unresolved childishness.

2) The skeletons in the closet are now on the clock.

Urging Innovation

ADAPT (or else): 1) What the leadership team *routinely* preaches to employees, not all of whom believe in evolution. 2) Thanks to the practice of reverse engineering, aspiring to be unimaginative in an innovative way.

BURN THE BOATS: Says the CEO, while watching from a distant yacht.

CREATIVE DESTRUCTION: 1) A business philosophy in favor of letting the dumpster fires burn bright. 2) A term its fans would abandon like a nuclear potato if they knew its originator, Joseph Schumpeter, basically agreed with Karl Marx that capitalism is bound to eat itself alive. 3) An approach endorsed by Schumpeterians, who oppose anything that works in practice if it doesn't also work in theory.

THINK OUTSIDE THE BOX: 1) A management command which fails to acknowledge that the "box" is really more like a coffin. 2) Any idea that is 2% to 4% different from what the company is currently doing. 3) When put into practice, a cliché that loosely translates into "My cubicle is making me claustrophobic, so I'm going out for a three-hour lunch."

XEROX®: A company that welcomes being a copycat.

Expansion That Will Blow up, Eventually

DIVERSIFICATION: The acquisition of a company whose name rhymes with yours.

GLOBALIZATION: When a U.S. based company opens a branch in Canada. There it quickly learns that while the dream of Canada was to combine American know-how, British politics, and French culture, in reality the country combines British know-how, American culture, and French politics.

LEVERAGE: 1) The hope of gaining a sustainable, unfair advantage without breaking a sweat. 2) If used as a verb preceding "synergy," expect 2 + 2 to suddenly equal 5.

VERTICAL INTEGRATION: 1) The first step toward creating a monopoly, which ensures that every part of the supply chain will be miserable at the same time. 2) The opportunity to right-size a workforce that consists of many mutually incompatible parts, not unlike the former Hapsburg Empire.

WE DON'T HAVE ENOUGH BOOTS ON THE GROUND: We haven't been able to find enough gullible, clueless people willing to do what we want. Fortunately, our plans are up in the air.

Incompetency (That Will Pull Others down, Too)

EXECUTIVE SUMMARY: 1) A way of helping those who make the most money read less. 2) A one-pager to help marketers and executives with ADD syndrome avoid breaking a mental sweat.

INNER CIRCLE: Those powerful enough to make the company go around and around, like a dog chasing its tail.

TAKING CREDIT: 1) A C-suite core competency. 2) What people who aren't good enough to do any real work excel at.

UPPER MANAGEMENT: The people who get to park closer to the front door than do either the company's visiting customers or those who are officially handicapped.

WE NEED TO WRAP OUR HEADS AROUND THIS: I'm management. Use small words and only a few of them. Pictures help.

Relying on a Low-Cost Labor Model

(the new) GIG ECONOMY: The trend of turning America into a nation of folk musicians with their guitar cases sitting open on the sidewalk.

LEAN AND MEAN: 1) Corporate poetry in its rawest form. 2) A steakhouse you don't favor.

LIVING WAGE: The minimum wage x gazillion.

PART-TIME: The likelihood of working 30 to 40 hours a week for 20 hours' worth of pay.

PAYCHECK: A reluctant deduction from the company's profit margin.

Addicted to Cost-Cutting (That Starts with Payroll)

LAY-OFFS: A once common business term for dismissal, arrived at by combining two words to ensure neither one makes sense. The term has now been replaced by "Reduction in Force," which has proven more effective because it makes people think about *Star Wars* instead of the Unemployment Office.

LIFETIME EMPLOYMENT: Say *what?*

(early) RETIREMENT: For lots of workers, whenever a new recession strikes.

SALARY: A life-preserver made of legal tender that attracts cost-cutting sharks.

SEVERANCE PACKAGES: Giving rank-and-file employees their own version of a golden parachute, minus the ripcord.

Finding Salvation in Technology & Outsourcing

AUTOMATION: 1) Staffing reductions that involve a plug-in cord. 2) The antonym for JOB SECURITY, i.e., the hazy, feel-good belief that one's position is safe despite overwhelming evidence to the contrary.

OUTSOURCING: A cost-cutting move that works great so long as you're the last-surviving member of your family that ever needs a job, you're the owner, and you don't mind learning to speak Mandarin.

REDUNDANT EMPLOYEE: 1) A weirdly normal designation in the age of outsourcing. 2) Rationalize. Remove. Repeat.

ROBOTS: 1) High-cost machines that replace low-wage people so that prices can ultimately be lower, though not low enough for those formerly employed to afford. 2) The kind of personnel that introverts prefer to manage.

SKILLSET: 1) Capabilities that fall into three categories: irrelevant, obsolete or imaginary. 2) Use "rich skillset" or "robust skillset" when referring to individuals over 45 years of age.

Having a Jaundiced Talent Management Perspective

COMMODITIES: Cheap goods easily obtained in massive qualities, ranging from copper, corn, coffee beans, pork bellies, and ferrous scrap metal to a company's labor force.

RANK-AND-YANK: The sequel to *Jaws*, specifically the scene in which the Mayor of Amity insists it's safe to go back into the water.

RESPECT: The opposite of contempt, and as such an increasingly quaint word unlikely to appear in the second edition of this fine book.

TERMINATION: 1) Getting rid of employees in a manner befitting a pest-control service. 2) In instances of early termination, a dismissal that always comes more quickly than the victim had any right to expect.

TURN-OVER: 1) Employees getting flipped like burgers, burnt on one side and raw with anger on the other. 2) The speed at which goods sell, minus the rate at which employees leave in a huff.

The HR Department as Unindicted Co-Conspirator

FLAT: 1) An organizational structure in which most middle managers get left for dead. Meanwhile, packs of wild dogs roam the hallways looking for a stray leader or two to bark at. 2) Our sales are downright *sh*tty*, but we need a better way to describe them in the annual report.

HUMAN CAPITAL: 1) Turning the HR department into a pawn shop. 2) The single most important asset of a corporation, hence the asset most quickly exchanged for a greater profit margin.

HUMAN RESOURCES: A department that exists so executives won't have to think about their "most important resource," i.e., personnel; with those at the top praised as "talent" and those at the bottom dismissed as "livewire" or "meatware."

INJUSTICE: The stench that every HR department tries to fumigate.

TISSUE LADY: 1) A condescending term that leaders use for the HR team they depend on to handle emotionally taxing situations like employees getting reprimanded, laid-off or forced to listen to a speech given by any of those same leaders. 2) A term used by those who grieve missing a putt.

Company Bravado

(the company) LOGO: A medieval coat-of-arms minus a sense of purpose or pretense of honor.

MISSION STATEMENTS: Companies feeding employees a diet of Wonder Bread®.

PRIDE: A company third in its category but the first to congratulate itself.

REPUTATION: The degree to which a company is well known for disregarding its customers.

TOP TIER: 1) Being the leading company in a category because you swallowed everybody else whole. 2) The beneficiary of an unexpected lift in sales, usually preceded by offers like "Buy one, get a carload free."

Self-Serving Presentations

CHARTS: 1) A crowd of numbers and geometrical shapes struggling to avoid asphyxiation. 2) Like the C-suite's office holders, vertical bar charts biased in favor of height.

CHRONIC FATIGUE: Being taken on a forced march through several PowerPoint presentations per day.

MANAGEMENT PORN: Any slide deck with either more than ten slides or a single slide with more than five bullet points, statistics or graphic elements—none of which have anything to do with reality.

RELIEF: The feeling you get when you realize nobody has spotted the inaccuracies (okay, *downright* lies) in your latest boardroom presentation.

VISUAL AIDS: Imagery meant to bring a deck of presentation slides back from the dead.

Rely on Jargon, Platitudes & Acronyms

ACRONYM SOUP

CYA in action

The acronym for
Three-Letter Acronyms
(yes, it's true)

Bad at Rallying the Troops (Poor Communication Skills)

BACK OF THE NET: In relying on sports analogies, the moment in a leader's speech when, rather than strike out again, he or she turns the triumph of scoring in soccer into business dribble instead.

(it's a) NO-BRAINER: Said by those exhibiting an instinctive grasp of the obvious.

PERFORMANCE (issues): Leaders trying to espouse empathy.

(corporate) SPEECHES: Prefabricated houses built using platitudes as crossbeams.

TALKING POINTS: 1) A series of non-answers to questions one doesn't want to address. A practice adopted from political campaigns, where candidates sound like they have a plan to fix everything for everyone without having to charge anybody anything. 2) The opposite of *feeling* points, which require some conviction.

Isolated & Seemingly beyond Reproach

(the) BOARD OF DIRECTORS: Well-paid, absentee landlords who insist they're not responsible for the plumbing.

HEADQUARTERS: Ego island.

POWER: The opportunity to do something wrong whenever one so desires. In CEOs, a tendency made worse by the fact that honest feedback usually travels horizontally, not vertically, in a corporate structure.

THERE'S NO "I" IN TEAM: But oddly enough, it crops up in both *executives* and *nepotism.*

UNTOUCHABLE: In India, a member of the lowest caste. In corporate life, the exact opposite.

Champions of a Dysfunctional Culture (Fit in or Else)

COMPANY CULTURE: 1) A cult you have to join or else you won't get any work done. 2) A synonym for office politics. 3) Bacteria that grows when people are forced to work together.

COMPANY UNIFORMS: Now say after me, "We are all individuals."

MANDATORY: A company policy as soft and pliable as a jack boot. 2) The "random" drug testing of employees, starting with anybody who doesn't walk, talk, and look like the CEO.

PROBLEMS: 1) Non-existent. Officially abolished in Corporate America by virtue of the Lollipop Act of 1957. 2) Sometimes referred to as "challenges" or "improvement opportunities" to sound less negative, e.g., turning the famous Apollo 13 spaceflight warning into "Houston, we have an improvement opportunity."

(corporate) RISK TAKERS: A subspecies about as welcome at HQ as an infestation of fire ants.

Mirror, Mirror on the Wall

MERITOCRACY: A mirror-tocracy reflecting the company's preference for hiring and promoting people who look, think, and act like the people already in charge.

WHO'S THE FAIREST OF THEM ALL?

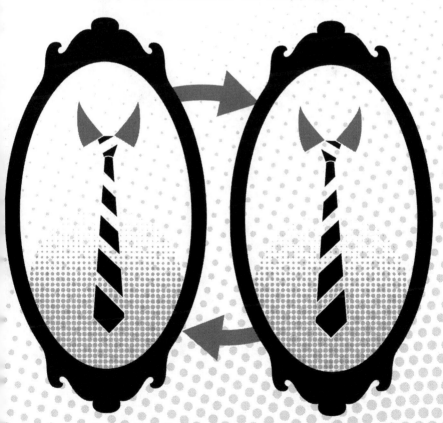

Bureaucracy Run Amuck

(the) APPROVAL PROCESS: 1) Also known as the *evisceration* process. 2) A way to delay taking action on your idea until the next company re-organization, at which point you'll no longer be around. 3) Middle managers discovering how hard they can get kicked for doing what they thought they were authorized to do. 4) Permission-based regression of an "idea of one" down the slippery slope of groupthink, facilitated by a committee of dilatory observers.

DEEP DIVE: Exploring the Great Barrier Reef of bureaucratic indifference.

INTEGRATED: An archaic way of saying "mash-up."

PYTHONS: Bloated bureaucracies capable of swallowing anything except the truth.

RED TAPE: Of benefit to victims by making it more difficult for them to do something which would have surely failed.

Telling Employees to Cheer up (or Else)

CASH BAR: A way of hosting a party that makes both the Finance and HR departments happy.

COMPANY HOLIDAY PARTIES: As good a reason as any to become an atheist.

EMPLOYEE RECOGNITION AWARDS: 1) A surefire way to kill the morale of everyone else and cause them to leave the company. 2) Justified as a means of boosting employee retention. 3) Gilding the lily by giving the company's best employees certificates "For Outstanding Achievement in the Field of Excellence."

EMPOWERMENT: 1) The opportunity to exercise free will as soon as you're told it's okay to do so, conditions permitting. 2) The fulcrum of companies' on-going efforts to crossbreed a mountain lion and a gerbil.

(being encouraged to) LEAN IN: The precursor to throwing up.

Sexism Abounds

BROPROPRIATION: 1) When a woman's valuable suggestion or creative idea gets plagiarized by a man who then blithely cashes the royalty check. 2) A phenomenon also known as hepeating or himitating.

GENDER GAP: As far as many if not most male executives are concerned, merely the defunct version of a famous retail chain serving binary people.

GLASS CEILING: The fate of women whose careers get sidelined by various postings, such as being named the captain of a cost-center senior management hopes to scuttle or else being put in charge of a branch office located somewhere between Outer Mongolia and Obscuristan.

GUT CHECK: The oblique way (male) leaders refer to emotions, conveniently bypassing the heart, which is regarded as a female organ.

GUYS: A way of greeting everybody in the office because, as American Express® proclaims, *member*ship has its privileges.

MANEL: A nondiverse (all-male) conference panel. Because really, we don't get to hear nearly enough about what white men think.

MOMMY-TRACK: The dead-end career path for many of those who take family responsibilities seriously because, after all, why would an organization *possibly* want to place in positions of authority people who truly care about others?

PAY DISCRIMINATION: Most often, a company-wide bias that privileges the ability to grow a beard over everything else.

(the) RECEPTIONIST: 1) Typically a woman who, odds are, may also be the smartest, most organized, and least well-paid person in the company. 2) The back-up assistant for female colleagues who get assigned most of the office housework, e.g., taking meeting notes, bringing refreshments, and planning social events.

SEXUAL INNUENDOS AND HARASSMENT: While innuendos involve pointless body-part references that belong in a bedroom, not a conference room, harassment may become the catalyst for mandatory training whereby (some) male employees learn that "harass" isn't actually two separate words.

Seemingly Blind to Racism & Inequality in General

DIVERSITY: 1) In senior management, a *short* white guy. 2) A term the C-suite highlights in the company's Values Statement, though without officially giving it the status of an orphan. 3) In wondering why there's not more progress, knowing that the answer is *white* in front of your face.

EQUALITY: 1) A goal evident in any *Star Trek* episode or movie. 2) A goal considered a form of science fiction in the hallways of corporate America.

LEVEL PLAYING FIELD: 1) The laughable concept that equal opportunity truly exists, regardless of gender or race. 2) Among executives, real concern about whether the club's polo grounds have any divots that will require attention before Sunday's match.

XENOPHOBIA: The single most valid reason for why the letter X should remain in the alphabet.

ZERO-TOLERANCE POLICY: A company's firm commitment to reject discrimination in whatever form it might take that threatens long-standing privileges.

Pampered & Self-Indulgent (Nothing Left for Others)

CHARISMATIC LEADER: Someone in search of a balcony.

800-POUND GORILLA: The enforcer of the Golden Rule, which states that whoever has the gold makes the rules.

EXECUTIVE DINING ROOM: Where egos get fed and become TOO BIG TO FAIL.

OUT OF STOCK: While it may be okay for shoppers not to find what they're looking for, a situation that executives won't tolerate when it comes to receiving their compensation packages.

QUALITY CONTROL: Ensuring that executives' golden parachutes have high thread counts.

Scandal-Ridden (Financial or Otherwise)

ADMIRATION: The feeling you have for leaders whom you never directly worked for.

APOLOGY LAUNDERING: Scandals that come out smelling rosy so that the company can remain filthy rich.

BORDERLINE DECISIONS: What leaders with borderline personalities do best.

SUSTAINABILITY: 1) Framing the elimination of paper bags with handles for shoppers as "taking one for Team Earth." 2) A term invoked by executives after the company installs energy-efficient windows at a facility where the carbon emissions are so high animals are dying in the forest nearby.

TRUST: 1) The emotion of business insofar as MBA program administrators and nuns are concerned. 2) A matter of family values meaning "my family, not yours." 3) An essential brand attribute (unless you're Facebook® or Amazon®, in which case your market share renders trust unnecessary).

Sticky Fingers

SCANDAL: Anything too big for a company to hide as usual.

TAKING THE DOWN ESCALATOR

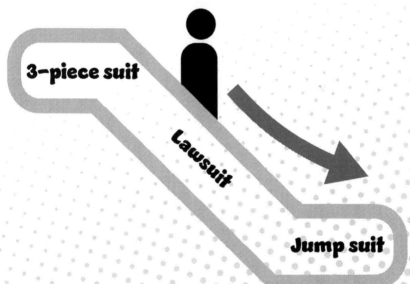

3-piece suit

Lawsuit

Jump suit

Financial Chicanery

ACQUIRE: A socially approved way to steal.

ASSETS: That which has not yet been misappropriated, misspent or simply stolen.

EMBEZZLEMENT: For those times when trickle-down economics doesn't fill the punch bowl quickly enough.

(corporate) EXPENSE ACCOUNTS: 1) The next, higher level of mastery after lying with statistics. 2) Money that might have gone to the company's bottom line helping to expand waistlines instead.

JUST-IN-TIME INVENTORY: A method to avoid paying vendors.

MONEY: A medium of exchange involving small coins, paper-thin banknotes, and really massive fraud.

PROFITABILITY: The best excuse for unethical behavior.

QUARTERLY EARNINGS: 1) A set of numbers derived from a combination of real data and judicious editing. 2) Company leaders giving science fiction a try.

STOCK BUYBACKS: Rather than invest in R & D, aka *the future*, company executives having the wisdom to invest in a much surer thing, namely their own greed.

WHITE-COLLAR CRIME: 1) Something likely to be committed above street-level and over the heads of most juries. 2) When a gun's safety lock is upgraded to a pair of locks on a leather briefcase.

Financial Mismanagement

BANKRUPTCY: A do-over. The corporate equivalent of a five-year-old kicking over the board when faced with the prospect of losing at checkers.

CASH COW: The part of the company herd that management mistakenly believes no longer merits feeding.

NEPOTISM: An inverse form of corporate Darwinism, whereby the corrupt and incompetent are declared the fittest so that they might accelerate the organization's downfall.

OUTCOME: Income already spent.

SAVINGS: Subject to the formula of potential earnings minus actual costs.

OTHER BUFFOONS

Investors

(a company's) ANNUAL REPORT: Glossy half-truths, widely distributed.

(the) ANNUAL STOCKHOLDERS MEETING: Another case of the powers-that-be granting themselves the power to grant themselves more power.

DIVIDENDS: The loot that companies give shareholders after firing the staff, cheapening the product, reducing the advertising budget, and moving offshore prior to declaring themselves to be good corporate citizens.

JUNK BONDS: 1) A purchase that allowed your financial advisor to send his or her children to schools you could scarcely afford then and surely cannot afford now. 2) Investment instruments that in singular form always introduces itself as "Bond, Junk Bond."

SHAREHOLDER RIGHTS: The inverse of sharecropper rights.

Bankers and the "Street"

ALONE: What banks won't give you when you need it most.

EARNINGS SURPRISE: A CEO and CFO together at the whipping post.

FUTURE EARNINGS: Sandcastles built by adults.

IPO (Initial Public Offering): Investment bankers salivating.

LABOR DAY: A federal holiday established in 1894 to honor the contributions of workers by permitting Wall Street bankers to take an extra day off.

Competitors, Entrepreneurs & Venture Capitalists

ARCHRIVAL: The company your company's executives hope to be hired by next.

BIG MONEY: Investors whose doctors describe them as being financially obese.

BURN RATE: Throwing bundles of cash overboard as fast as one can to stay afloat.

DISRUPTED: 1) When your company's prime rib steak gets abruptly turned into hamburger by an upstart. 2) A new monopoly in the making.

ELEVATOR PITCH: The ability to deliver a comprehensive lie in less than one minute.

ENTREMANURE: What you often end up with when you strike out on your own.

EQUITY: 1) A start-up company giving shares to anyone who can make something out of nothing. 2) The reason people stay at unbearable companies.

INTELLECTUAL PROPERTY (IP): 1) I think, therefore I own.™ 2) A proprietary, secret-sauce methodology used by a company serving indigestible food.

MONETIZE: Along with scalability, entrepreneurs other favorite word when playing Scrabble®.

VENTURE CAPITALISTS: 1) Billionaire gamblers. 2) The discovery that pythons are actually herd animals.

The Government

(seeking a) BAILOUT: The feeding of corporate gluttons.

(the) CHECK IS IN THE MAIL: 1) Financial engineering that tries to make the U.S. postage system into a co-conspirator. 2) In business, similar to "I'll still respect you in the morning."

CORNERING THE MARKET: 1) Corner-office speak for "The lawyers will help us avoid an antitrust action." 2) Aided by "getting the rules right," i.e., making a mockery of antitrust laws.

CORPORATE TAXES: The inspiration for various financial magic tricks, including U.S. headquarter buildings shrink-wrapped to match the size of post office boxes in Bermuda.

FUD (Fear, Uncertainty, Doubt): A new government agency that specializes in only saying "No."

On the Small Screens inside Their Heads

INDUSTRY ASSOCIATION: A group that takes notes while watching episodes of *The Sopranos*.

FAVORITE TV SHOWS

IT Dept.
THE TWILIGHT ZONE

VENTURE CAPITALISTS
HOUSE OF CARDS

Salespeople
BEAVIS AND BUTT-HEAD

The Accounting Department & Outside Auditors

AUDIT: The business world's version of a colonoscopy.

FRAUD: 1) What quarterly reports and expense accounts have in common. 2) An accounting term denoting creativity and innovation.

NEGATIVE GROWTH: Oxymoron that means "losing money," though it sounds so much better in annual reports and presentations thanks to having the word "growth" in it.

OPERATING COSTS: 1) Fictitious numbers, usually inflated, that allow a company to balance its books and turn a profit by lowering its tax burden. 2) Surgeon's fees.

NET-90: A client's Finance department deciding to pay a vendor in three months' time because the odds are the vendor will be bankrupt by then.

(a company's) PROFIT-AND-LOSS STATEMENT: A sailboat that tips from side to side, depending on whether the wind is coming from Wall Street or the IRS.

PROFITS: 1) The money assumed to be left over after the customer pays for the product, the overhead is deducted, and the head of Finance agrees to cook the books to reflect strategic "success." 2) A place on a P & L sheet reserved for hope but usually occupied by regret. 3) Money made by someone who doesn't deserve it, at the expense of another person who does.

RED INK: The business equivalent of coughing up blood.

REVENUE PROJECTIONS: 1) A situation in which well-presented fantasies are applauded by those who will later distance themselves. 2) The business equivalent of visiting a psychic.

VENDORS: The people a client company screws first, before it gets around to customers and creditors.

The IT Department & Technology in General

CHATBOTS: Automated website attendants about as responsive as your average husband if asked his opinion of pasta seasoning while he's watching a sporting event on TV.

HELP DESK: Where one goes to hear "Have you tried rebooting your system?"

PROGRAMMER: Someone who solves a problem you didn't know you had in a way you don't understand.

SMART MACHINES: Since the Greek goddess Circe could turn men into pigs (hardly a novel feat), what might Apple's® Siri and Amazon's® Alexa prove capable of?

VAPORWARE: 1) Software so cutting edge it may never exist. 2) That which in an earlier era would have simply been called a *lie*.

The Research & Development Department

EASY: A promise made by assembly-kit instructions impossible to decipher.

GUARANTEED: Disappointment.

LIFECYCLE: 1) Within a company, a series of product development failures to which marketing gets appended. 2) For customers, a cycle that involves being at first too young to afford a product, and then too busy to discern its merits before, finally, becoming too old to recognize the product at all.

MADE IN AMERICA: The packaging and the label were added here in the States.

R & D: The department where all good product ideas go to get pummeled and revert to last year's model.

The Legal Department & Outside Counsel

BILLABLE HOURS: The ability of lawyers to achieve 300-hour work weeks without violating the laws of physics.

CONTRACT: 1) How the Purchasing department prevents employees from trying anything new. 2) Legalese for a carefully drafted document of Best Intentions. 3) The business version of New Year's resolutions, i.e., that which is quickly created, quickly discarded, and uncomfortable to revisit six months later.

CORPORATE LAWYERS: Conspirators who wear pin-striped suits rather than prison garb with the same black-and-white color scheme running horizontally instead.

(a company's) EMAIL TRAIL: An opposing attorney's best friend.

(my) FINAL OFFER: The start of serious negotiations.

(a company's) LEGAL DEPARTMENT: Experts in everything illegal.

NDA (Non-Disclosure Agreement): 1) The mistaken belief that one's intellectual property is worth something just because one paid a fortune to have a lawyer draw up a paper which says so. 2) A promise not to tell a friend or two.

SEPARATION AGREEMENTS: Employees on their way out the door agreeing to receive what they're legally entitled to provided they give up their legal rights.

WHISTLE-BLOWER: The fool not in on the scheme.

WORKMAN'S COMP: The extra money you get for doing the job poorly.

Pricing: Accountants & Marketers Butt Heads

FREE: Something customers will most definitely pay for but will never guess how.

NO MONEY DOWN: 1) A distraction ploy leading to the repossession of the product from downcast and humiliated buyers, with the real action being the goal of keeping the factory up and running. 2) A trickle-down economic model in which all the money stays at the top.

PRICE BREAK: A company's way of shouting "May day, may day."

PRICE GOUGING: A tactic endorsed by colleagues who are the kind of friends your mother warned you about.

PRICE HIKE: Telling the company's most loyal customers to take a different path.

Advertising Agencies

HOW THE GAME GETS PLAYED

ADVERTISING AGENCIES: Fervent believers in an 11th Commandment "God gave you eyes, plagiarize."

STOPPING POWER: Advertising that grabs consumers' attention by squeezing it to death.

STORY BOARDS: Something for younger employees to carry to a client meeting so they don't look inexperienced, pointless, and unbillable.

The Marketing Department

BRAND LINKAGE: Greenlighting funny commercials that make everyone laugh. Unfortunately, since the company isn't named Jerry Seinfeld, nobody remembers the sponsor.

(the) COMPANY TAGLINE: A slogan with the life span of a gnat.

DIGITAL TRANSFORMATION: 1) When your company finally learns what TikTok® is. 2) Taking one's existing, wasteful advertising methods and plugging them in *exactly as is* online.

EMAIL BLASTS: 1) Spam scientifically designed to avoid the spam folder. 2) Sending unwanted information to the indifferent people who populate irrelevant lists generated by a nobody who got everybody's email addresses from an unlisted service company. 3) Subtweeting for old people.

HIGH PRODUCTION VALUES: Advertising with the sheen of an oil slick.

MARKETING: The science of guessing right.

PERSUASION: The fond hope that a 30-second TV spot can overcome a lifetime of buyer's regret.

PLAINTIFF: The fifth "P" of marketing.

PROBLEM/SOLUTION (format): In pharmaceutical TV commercials forced to disclose the possible side effects of taking the drug, the promise to save your life by setting your hair on fire.

STICKY: A metaphor purporting that a website's visitor is an insect, a webpage is flypaper, and once the two are conjoined in virtual fashion, then a relationship has been joyfully consummated.

Consultants & Vendors in General

CHANGE AGENT: A confirmed bachelor.

DURU: A management guru who actually gets something done.

ESTIMATE: 1) A vendor testing the waters to see how much of a bath your company is willing to take. 2) Guessing at the prospect's ability and willingness to pay for what they don't need but now want.

HOLISTIC: I have no idea what I'm talking about but it's important for you to know that I have a MBA.

MANAGING EXPECTATIONS: Telling the client small lies over time, rather than one big lie at the end of the project.

Market Research & Data Analytics

BIG DATA: 1) A hippopotamus-sized version of a cat's hairball, complete with every entry your company has ever logged *minus* the one that would have won the next lawsuit: 2) A resource for finding a pattern that proves your point. 3) Using statistics to convince you there's a pattern you can't see in something you can't understand.

CUSTOMER FEEDBACK: Information nobody wants to hear that has been gathered by people nobody wants to know, using a survey form nobody wants to answer.

FORECASTING: 1) The use of charts to make a guess. 2) A way of getting managers to commit to impossible targets.

MARKET RESEARCH: Should hypotheses be confirmed, proof of the client's wisdom. Otherwise, a waste of money for a study lacking a representative sample.

SURVEY RESULTS: 1) The outcome of a long, careful process of guiding participants to an inevitable conclusion. 2) A vice president's pet idea gaining validation after the questionnaire is changed to ask participants how much they like the idea on a scale from 9 to 10.

The Sales Department

BANG FOR THE BUCK: 1) The street version of saying "ROI." 2) A dubious travel expense that gets assigned to "entertainment," e.g., the strip club that a salesman claims was the only place still serving food at that hour.

(the room's) MINIBAR: The high-water mark of capitalism. Invented by the hotel industry to punch holes in corporate expense accounts by charging tired business travelers inflated amounts of money for morsels of alcohol and chocolate so tiny they have to be gift-wrapped by elves.

PESSIMISM: Your best estimate of how well the product will sell.

PROSPECTS: 1) Someone with a pulse. 2) People with targets on their foreheads. 3) The next person to say "No."

SALES PIPELINE: 1) The basis for reviewing the organization's upcoming revenue potential which, while vital to bankers and shareholders, is a report prepared by a group of people who have difficulty finding and recording their last receipt from Denny's®. 2) The list of companies the sales reps tell you they're calling on with "real" potential, even though some of the firms are now out of business.

SOFT SELL: 1) What precedes the hard sell if the prospect says "No." 2) A gunman fumbling with his holster.

(gaining) TRACTION: How the business development team describes the benefit of picking up a $1,000 restaurant tab.

TRADE SECRETS: 1) What people first tweet about after their non-disclosure agreements expire. 2) What salespeople tell their bosses they learned about their competitors at a trade show, even though a Google® search did the trick.

TRADE SHOW: The place to meet new customers and avoid dissatisfied ones.

UPSELL: Getting customers to purchase insurance policies that guarantee their extended warranties will remain valid.

Customers Last & Least? Too Often True

BUYER'S REGRET: The cul-de-sac in which the customer's journey comes to an end.

CALL MENU OPTIONS: The opportunity to scream "Representative" into your phone repeatedly.

CASHIER: The spectacle of a person unhappy about being handed money all day long.

CRM (Customer Relationship Management): Stalking.

CUSTOMER CENTRIC: Figuring out what large group of people a business can target to better sell what's already in its inventory.

DIY (Do It Yourself): Letting customers make the mistakes because it's much cheaper than making them oneself.

EVANGELISTS: 1) The loyal customers everyone strives to have despite knowing that they're about as common as leprechauns. 2) The people on staff assigned to "special projects."

SIZING GUIDE: 1) A diplomatic way of letting potential customers know they've gained a lot of weight. 2) Also see ONE SIZE FITS ALL, aka a line of clothing designed by the makers of Glad® trash bags.

(we're experiencing) UNUSUALLY HIGH CALL VOLUMES:
1) The admission that *No one showed up to work today.* Or . . . *We can't find them. We'll be back to you when and if we can.* 2) The eternal mystery of why this predicament never results in greater-than-usual staffing levels.

YOUR CALL IS VERY IMPORTANT TO US: And now here in full, while you wait, is Beethoven's Ninth Symphony.

Apple Sauce, Not Apple Pie

SORRY FOR ANY INCONVENIENCE YOU MAY HAVE EXPERIENCED: Gaslighting, corporate style.

Acknowledgments

Roughly a third of these diabolical definitions came in turn from myself, Howard Moskowitz, and the combined efforts of the other, 50 contributors to this book. Most prolific among them were Marti Barletta, Mark Botros, Bob Bundy, Charles Christian, Tim Houlihan, Blaine Parker, Annie Pettit, Andrew Tarvin, Lynn Taylor, and especially Kelly Smith and Rico Paul Vallejos. Thank you all. I also want to thank Jerry Lee, Annie Pettit, Rico Paul Vallejos, and John Burns for helping me winnow down which entries to ultimately include. Finally but not least, I'm grateful to my wife, Karen Bernthal, for turning my clumsy illustrations into something far sweeter.

Preface

Robert Kaufelt: capitalism (1); Rico Paul Vallejos: capitalism (2).

Chapter 1: Your Own Foibles

Chris Andruss: thought leader (2-3); David Barash: commuting (2); Marti Barletta: I'm swamped (3), MBA (2), work/life balance (2); Mark Botros: shelf life, short-circuit, work stoppages; Bob Bundy: work/life balance (1), workshops; Charles Christian: MBA (1), sexual misconduct; Andy Cohen: optimism (2); Tim Houlihan: burning the candle at both ends (2), on-the-job training; Nika Kabiri: empathy (1-2); Brian Ketchel: thought leader (1); Art Markman: imposter syndrome, job interview; Dave Mathias: debrief; Don Oehlert: pension (1); Blaine Parker, jump the shark, moving the cheese; Annie Pettit: framed diplomas; lunch break (2); Wes Schaeffer: early adopters (1-2); Kelly Smith: altruism, change, early adopters (3), early bird, excuses (2), honesty, perks; Caroline Stokes: you're fired; John Sweeney: training (2); Andrew Tarvin: burning the candle at both ends (1); Lynn Taylor: eye-rolling, passion, thought leader (4); Rico Paul Vallejos: epic, resume.

(2), I'll get back to you (1), partnering, screening my calls (1); Deny Soto: send me a clean email; Caroline Stokes: touching base (1); John Sweeney: brainstorming (2); Lynn Taylor: co-sourcing; Rico Paul Vallejos: ideation (3), I'll get back to you (3), let's ballpark this, organic (1); Mike Wittenstein: bless your heart (1).

Chapter 4: Executive Blunders

Chris Andruss: lay-offs; Mitch Anthony: company culture (3); David Barash: paycheck; Marti Barletta: adapt (2), integrated, level playing field (1), sexual innuendos and harassment; Mark Botros: quarterly earnings (2), right-sizing (2), vertical integration (1); Christina Binkley: outcome; Amy Bucher: trust (3); Bob Bundy: bankruptcy, realignment (1), taking credit (1), top tier (2), upper management, we need to wrap our heads around this; Bradley Charbonneau: we don't have enough boots on the ground (1); Charles Christian: globalization, relief; Cary Cooper: apology laundering, mergers and acquisitions (1); Tim Houlihan: (the) approval process (3), sustainability (2), taking credit (2); W. Brad Johnson & David G. Smith: bropropriation, manel, receptionist (2); Niki Kabiri: skillset; Robert Kaufelt: empowerment (1), just-in-time inventory, profitability; Michael Kerr: think outside the box (3); Brian Ketchel: employee recognition awards (3); Jerry Lee: employee recognition awards (1-2); Nick Morgan: downsizing (1), five-year plan (1); Elissa Moses: charts (2); Sharon Mowen: family business (2); Don Oehlert: downsizing (2), lifetime employment, talking points (1); Blaine Parker: approval process (1), borderline decisions, creative destruction (2); Annie Pettit: receptionist; B. Joseph Pine II: human resources, vision (1); Paul Schuster: gig economy, right-sizing (1); Kelly Smith: automation, big picture, executive dining room, gender gap, headquarters, redundant employee (2), robots (2), trendspotting; Dan Smolen: human capital (1); Caroline Stokes: company culture (1-2), diversity (2), equality, tissue lady (1); John Sweeney: think outside the box (2); Andrew Tarvin: admiration, (the) approval process (4), cash bar; Lynn Taylor: right-sizing (3), streamline (1), there is no "I" in team; Rico Paul Vallejos: redundant employee (1), sexual innuendos and harassment, turn-over (2); Thomas Wedell-Wedellsborg: problems (2).

Chapter 5: Other Buffoons

Chris Andruss: contract (1); Mitch Anthony: entremanure; David Barash: Labor Day, profits (3); Marti Barletta: prospects (2); Mark Botros: revenue projections, venture capitalists (1); Bob Bundy: big data (1), chatbots, (the) check is in the mail (2), contract (3), evangelists (2), prospects (1), sales pipeline (1), trade secrets (1); Simon Chadwick: venture capitalists (2); Charles Christian: (the room's) minibar; Laura Dragne: programmer; Tim Houlihan: (the) check is in the mail (1), forecasting (2), (gaining) traction, R & D, sales pipeline (2), trade secrets (2); Nika Kabiri: evangelists (1); Steve Lance: alone; Jerry Lee: marketing; Elissa Moses: market research; Don Oehlert: upsell; Blaine Parker: bang for the buck (2), buyer's regret; junk bonds (2), sticky; Annie Pettit: cashier, (the) company tagline, email blasts (3), fraud (1), free, no money down (2); Kelly Smith: help desk, intellectual property (1), NDA (2), price break; Andrew Tarvin: bang for the buck (1), digital transformation (1), forecasting (1); Lynn Taylor: equity (2), negative growth; Rico Paul Vallejos: cornering the market (1), DIY, elevator pitch, email blasts (1), fraud (2), legal department, lifecycle, made in America, no money down (1), operating costs (2), plaintiff (1); Thomas Wedell-Wedellsborg: Net-90.

About the Contributors

Chris Andruss is a veteran strategic brand communicator and marketing copywriter. A native of Chicago, he eventually moved to Cincinnati to work on a variety of well-known consumer brands.

Mitch Anthony is the author of 18 books, including *The New Retiremental- ity—Planning Your Life and Living Your Dream . . . at Any Age*. His programs on retirement/life issues are now in use by hundreds of corporations worldwide.

David Barash is a research scientist and author who spent 43 years as a professor of psychology at the University of Washington in Seattle. Besides over 240 peer-reviewed scientific papers, he's written or co-written 41 books.

Marti Barletta is the foremost authority on marketing to the world's big spenders—women. Her books have been published in 23 languages. Her lat- est book is *Selling to Affluent Women: Face-to-Face with Today's Big Spenders*.

Christina Binkley is a journalist and author of the *New York Times* best- seller *Winner Takes All*. A former staff writer and columnist at the *Wall Street Journal*, she contributes to *WSJ Magazine* and *The New Yorker*, and is an editor-at-large at *Vogue Business*.

Eszter Boczan is a neuroscientist who has helped FMCG, retail and technology clients use behavioral science measurements. Besides con- ducting research at Kantar, she reviews scientific publications for business applications.

Mark Botros is a management consultant and the host of the podcast *Live Works*. He is an international speaker, researcher, and advisor, including to over 300 organizations over the past 25 years.

Amy Bucher, PhD, is the Vice President of Behavior Design at Lirio. She previously worked at Mad*Pow, CVS Health, and Johnson & Johnson, and is the author of *Engaged: Designing for Behavior Change*.

Bob Bundy is a Vice President of Business Development, following roles as an organizational president, vice president of sales, vice president of product development, and managing director. His career has taken him around America.

Jamie Burrows hosts a video podcast, *Remotely Entertaining*, while working in digital marketing. His latest project is editing a book that chronicles the literary relationship between Archibald MacLeish and William Heyen.

Simon Chadwick is Managing Partner of the management consulting firm Cambiar LLC. He's a Fellow of the Market Research Society and the author of *For the People: A Citizen's Manifesto to Shaping Our Nation's Future*.

Bradley Charbonneau is the co-author of *Every Single Day: Daily Habits to Create Unstoppable Success, Achieve Goals Faster, and Unleash Your Extraordinary Potential*. He's also the host of the podcast *Repossible*.

Chris Carlson is a professional actor, attorney, and entrepreneur. He founded the communication consultancy NarrativePros to help others connect with audiences as he has on stage, screen, radio, and on corporate campuses across the country.

Charles Christian is an English barrister and Reuters correspondent turned writer, podcaster, radio show host, and award-winning tech journalist covering folklore, urban myths, rock music, and pop culture for his weekly *Weird Tales Radio Show*.

Andy Cohen is a *New York Times* Notable author. His latest book, *Challenge Your Assumptions, Change Your World*, explores the decision-making process to achieve better outcomes and improve critical thinking.

Cary Cooper, CBE, is a professor of Organizational Psychology and Health at the Manchester Business School in England. He's the author/editor of over 250 books, a former president of the British Academy of Management, and holds the title of CBE (Commander of the Most Excellent Order of the British Empire), which is given by her majesty the Queen for extraordinary contributions to society.

Laura Dragne is a PR professional and a supporter of social involvement actions. She's a graduate of Social Communication and Public Relations at the University of Bucharest, Romania.

Mark Goulston, MD, is a former UCLA professor of psychiatry, TEDx speaker, and the best-selling author of *Just Listen* and *Why Cope When You Can Heal?* Mark is also the inventor of Surgical Empathy and hosts the *My Wakeup Call* podcast.

Tim Houlihan is the founder and chief behavioral strategist of Behavior-Alchemy, a consultancy whose clients include non-profits and *Global 1000* firms. Tim's other activities include co-hosting *Behavioral Grooves*, a podcast with listeners in over 120 countries.

Brad Johnson is a professor of psychology in the Department of Leadership, Ethics and Law at the U.S. Naval Academy, and a faculty associate in the Graduate School of Education at Johns Hopkins University. He's the co-author of *Good Guys: How Men Can Be Better Allies for Women in the Workplace*.

Nika Kabiri, JD, PhD, is a Decision Science expert and business consultant. She teaches Decision Science at the University of Washington and is the co-author of *Money off the Table: Decision Science and the Secret to Smarter Investing*.

Robert Kaufelt was the proprietor of Murray's Cheese. He lives in Greenwich Village with his wife and three children.

Michael Kerr is a Hall of Fame speaker whose *Inspiring Workplaces* blog has been listed as one of the top-30 workplace blogs in the world. Michael is also the author of eight books, including *The Humor Advantage* and *The Jerk-Free Workplace*.

Pamela Knudsen is the founder of Brand Nature, a cultural insights and strategy consultancy. Its mission is to uncover 'outlier' human insights and link them to commercial factors in order to deliver fully-crafted strategies for brands seeking novel guidance.

Brian Ketchel is an IT professional who assists businesses to improve logistics processes through the use of technology. Brian is a resident and native of the Minneapolis/St. Paul area, where he runs a private consulting practice.

Steve Lance is the co-author of *The Little Blue Book of Advertising* and a three-time Emmy Award winner who has been fired from some of both the best and worst advertising agencies and television networks in the business.

Jerry Lee is a legendary radio broadcaster who for decades ran WBEB in Philadelphia. As a philanthropist, Jerry has been Knighted by King Gustav XVI of Sweden for establishing the Stockholm Prize in Criminology and has received a Private Sector Initiative award from former President Ronald Reagan.

Art Markman, PhD, is a Professor of Psychology and Marketing at the University of Texas at Austin. Besides authoring books, Art writes blogs for *Psychology Today* and *Fast Company*, and has a radio show/podcast called *Two Guys on Your Head*.

Dave Mathias helps leaders and organizations be more customer-focused and data-driven to deliver better customer experiences. He's the founder of Beyond the Data and author of the *Go Beyond the Data* newsletter and podcast.

Dr. Nick Morgan is one of America's top communication theorists and coaches. He's written for Fortune 50 CEOs, political and education leaders, and has coached people to give Congressional testimony, appear on TV, and deliver TED talks.

Elissa Moses is the CEO of BrainGroup Global, a Partner in Hark Connect and Bellwether Citizen Response, and a member of the faculty at Columbia University. Elissa was previously the CEO of Global Neuro and Behavioral Science at Ipsos.

Sharon Mowen is a veteran market research consultant, a career she stumbled into after completing a PhD in motivational psychology at the University of Exeter, UK. Corporate America's foibles have provided fodder for her contributions to this book.

Don Oehlert is the Managing Partner of eCareerCoaching.com, LLC. Don has been a career coach for over 17 years, helping over 700 leaders. A prolific blogger, Don has also authored *The Executive's Guide to Job Search* and a *Companion Workbook*.

Blaine Parker is the author of several business books, including *Billion-Dollar Branding: Brand Your Small Business Like a Big Business and Make Great Things Happen*. Other activities include being an advertising consultant and a voiceover performer.

David Perry has been nicknamed the 'Rogue Recruiter' by the *Wall Street Journal*. He's the managing partner of Perry-Martel International, a top North American executive recruiting firm, and the author of several search-related books.

Annie Pettit, PhD., FCRIC, is a research writer and methodologist, a keen supporter of research standards and ethics, and an advocate for diversity and equity. On a side note, Annie admits to suffering from Ukulele Acquisition Syndrome.

B. Joseph Pine II is the co-founder of Strategic Horizons LLP and co-author of *The Experience Economy: Competing for Customer Time, Attention, and Money*. He's been a visiting scholar or lecturer at institutions ranging from the MIT Design Lab to the University of Amsterdam and Columbia University.

Wes Schaeffer is The Sales Whisperer®, a reassuringly-expensive copy-writer, and a marketing automation expert. He is the author of 2.5 books, including *The Sales Whisperer Way*, and hosts both *The Sales Podcast* and *The CRM Sushi Podcast*.

Paul Samuel Schuster holds master's degrees in business communications and clinical social work. First as a marketer and now as a psychotherapist, the through-line has been his interest in the unconscious influences on human behavior.

David Smith is an associate professor of sociology in the College of Leadership and Ethics at the U.S. Naval War College. He's the co-author of *Good Guys: How Men Can Be Better Allies for Women in the Workplace*.

Kelly Smith is a serial entrepreneur, writer, and creative director who has spent his career in advertising, branding, and design. Since 2017, Kelly has led Thinkhaus Idea Factory, which specializes in creating brand experiences.

Dan Smolen is a podcaster and workforce advocate. Dan ended a successful 20-year-long executive search career to produce and host *The Dan Smolen Podcast*, which helps listeners pursue a future devoted to doing meaningful work.

Deny Soto is a marketer in Toronto with a career spanning various roles in strategy, research, and advertising. She's a middle child who can see issues from different perspectives—an ability that hasn't helped with handling her four-year-old.

Caroline Stokes is the CEO of FORWARD. She's an award-winning leadership coach, the author of *Elephants Before Unicorns: Emotionally Intelligent HR Strategies to Save Your Company*, and the podcast host of *The Emotionally Intelligent Recruiter*.

John Sweeney isn't notable because he owns the nation's oldest comedy theatre; because a quote from his first book appeared on millions of Starbucks coffee cups; or because he danced shirtless on national television, earning him "Fan of the Year" accolades from *The Today Show*. The reason is his speaking and training programs.

Andrew Tarvin is the CEO of Humor That Works, a leadership development company whose clients have included IBM, the UN, and the FBI. Andrew has been featured in the *Wall Street Journal, Inc.*, and *Fast Company*, and his TEDx talk has been viewed more than seven million times.

Lynn Taylor is a workplace expert and the author of *Tame Your Terrible Office Tyrant: How to Manage Childish Boss Behavior & Thrive in Your Job*. She's also a regular "Work" blogger for *Psychology Today*.

Rico Paul Vallejos is an award-winning writer, translator, transcreator, and copy editor of advertising and poetry in English and Spanish. He founded and served as the Editor-in-Chief of *La Voz de La Plaza*, an award-winning national publication; helped launch *La Voz Latina*; and is a Trustee Emeritus at Hamline University.

ABOUT THE CONTRIBUTORS

Thomas Wedell-Wedellsborg is the author of *What's Your Problem? To Solve Your Toughest Problems, Change the Problems You Solve*. His work has been featured in *The Economist*, and *HR Magazine* has ranked him as being a "Top 20 International Thinker."

Mike Wittenstein is a consultant, speaker, and former IBM eVisionary helping leaders introduce change. Mike and his Storyminers team use experience design and stories so clients' employees buy-in to strategies quickly and profitably.

About the Authors

Dan Hill, PhD, got his start as a writer by sharing his political satire columns with Art Buchwald when he was 14 years old. His writings were noted with commendation in three editions of *The Best American Essays* following his education at St. Olaf College, Oxford University, Brown University, and Rutgers University. He's the author of eight books, including *Emotionomics,* which was an *Advertising Age* top 10 must-read book in 2009 and features a foreword by Sam Simon, co-creator of *The Simpsons.* In 1998, Dan founded Sensory Logic, Inc., whose clients represent over 50% of the world's top 100 advertisers. Besides speaking to audiences in more than 25 countries, Dan has had media appearances ranging from ABC's "Good Morning, America" to NBC's "The Today Show," CNN, Fox, MSNBC, ESPN, and the Tennis Channel. Dan was also a regular guest on PBS's "Mental Engineering" show, hailed by Bill Moyers as "the most interesting weekly half hour of social commentary and criticism on television." In print, Dan has received front-page coverage in the *New York Times* and was a columnist for Reuters during the 2016 presidential race. Nowadays he hosts the podcast *Dan Hill's EQ Spotlight,* which appears on the New Books Network (NBN), the world's largest book review platform with over 1.7 million downloads monthly.

Howard Moskowitz is a legendary product market researcher, experiential psychologist, and inventor of world-class market research technologies used by virtually every company that matters. Howard earned his PhD in experimental psychology from Harvard University. In 2004, he was the subject of a *New Yorker* article by Malcolm Gladwell, "The Ketchup Conundrum," which became the basis for Gladwell's TED talk entitled "Choice, Happiness, and Spaghetti Sauce." In 2014, Howard founded Mind Genomics Associates to investigate how people think about aspects of their daily lives. In addition to over 400 scientific articles about the minds of consumers, Howard has written/edited 28 books, a roster that features the very popular book *Selling Blue Elephants.*

More from Dan Hill

Books – Other recent books, full of visuals, consist of the following:

Famous Faces Decoded: A Guidebook for Reading Others. This emotional intelligence primer covers seven core emotions and 23 facial expressions that reveal those emotions. Serving as examples are 173 U.S. celebrities and the emotional tendencies that characterize them.

Two Cheers for Democracy: How Emotions Drive Leadership Style. This book identifies emotional patterns that correlate to whether U.S. presidents have been effective in office; how well the candidates performed in presidential debates; and the degree to which 79 foreign leaders proved to be autocratic or democratic in their governing style.

First Blush: People's Intuitive Reactions to Famous Art. This is the largest study ever done involving art and eye-tracking. In all, 96 participants viewed 88 notable art works on-screen to learn where precisely they looked and how they felt about what they were seeing based on the synchronized use of facial coding analysis.

Talks – Whether for events like leadership off-site summits, national sales meetings or a company's lunch-and-learn lecture series (in-person or virtually), Dan can cover a wide range of topics. Options include: AI, EQ and upskilling to join the 5th Industrial Revolution; how to enhance trust to optimize the customer experience; and the secrets to creating effective marketing visuals. To learn more, visit **www.sensorylogic.com** or contact Dan at **dhill@sensorylogic.com**.

Made in the USA
Columbia, SC
20 September 2024

42697926R00087